THE POWER OF SELF-AWARENESS IN THE RETAIL INDUSTRY

NaToya Champion

Copyright © 2024 by NaToya Champion
All rights reserved. No part of this publication may be reproduced,
distributed, or transmitted in any form or by any means, including
photocopying, recording, or other electronic or mechanical methods,
without the prior written permission of the publisher, except in the case
of brief quotations embodied in critical reviews and certain other
noncommercial uses permitted by copyright law.

Dedication

I am deeply grateful to the remarkable individuals who have guided me on my journey toward self-awareness.

To my parents, whose unwavering prayers provided the foundation for my growth.

To my "Dream Team", Ryan (Shelby), Courtney, Rebecca, Tony, Anthony C, Eric F. and Shanesty, your candid advice and constant encouragement have helped me navigate through life's challenges with confidence and clarity.

To the "Wolfpack", each of you made me better!

To Terry "T. Nannie" and Amber, your wisdom and insightful conversations have been invaluable in helping me understand my strengths and weaknesses. Your belief in my potential pushed me to strive for self-improvement.

To "The Girls", April, Amy, Donna and Vickie, your friendship was what I needed and I'm incredibly thankful for you.

To my mentors, Agustin G., Jarred C., Kelvin B., Laura R., Tracy W., Annie W., thank you for taking a chance on me and thank you for being inclusive. You opened doors so that I could walk in.

To my children, Shekinah, Zachary, Alexia and Christian, thank you for your patience with "mommy". I love you.

Each of you has played a crucial role in my journey, and for that, I am eternally thankful. Your impact on my life is immeasurable, and I am honored to have you as part of my story.

With heartfelt gratitude,
NaToya

Contents

1. Introduction   1
2. The Fundamentals Of Self Awareness   5
3. The Impact Of Self-Awareness On Career Growth   11
4. Overcoming Blind Spots   19
5. Self-Awareness In Leadership   31
6. Cultural And Gender Perspectives On Self-Awareness   39
7. The Journey Of Self-Discovery And Continuous Improvement   49
8. Conclusion   59

About the Author   61

Introduction

Self-awareness is the ability to introspect and understand one's own thoughts, emotions, and behaviors. It involves being conscious of how you perceive yourself and how others perceive you. In personal development, self-awareness plays a crucial role as it serves as the foundation for growth and improvement.

One of the key aspects of self-awareness is self-reflection, which is the ability to examine your thoughts, feelings, and actions objectively. By being self-aware, you can identify your strengths and weaknesses, enabling you to make informed decisions and take actions that align with your values and goals. Self-awareness also enhances emotional intelligence, which is the ability to recognize and manage your own emotions, as well as understand and influence the emotions of others. This is particularly important in personal development as it allows you to navigate social interactions effectively and build meaningful relationships.

In the context of personal development, self-awareness enables you to:

- **Identify areas for improvement:** By understanding your strengths and weaknesses, you can focus on developing areas that need improvement, leading to personal and professional growth.
- **Enhance self-confidence:** Self-awareness allows you to have a realistic view of yourself, which can boost your self-confidence and self-esteem.
- **Improve decision-making:** Being aware of your values, beliefs, and goals can help you make decisions that are aligned with your true self, leading to more fulfilling outcomes.
- **Strengthen relationships:** Understanding your own emotions and behaviors can help you empathize with others and build stronger, more meaningful relationships.

Self-awareness plays a crucial role in career advancement, particularly in the dynamic and customer-centric environment of the retail industry. In the context of career advancement, self-awareness is essential because it enables individuals to identify their strengths, weaknesses, values, and goals. This self-understanding is particularly beneficial in the retail industry, where interpersonal skills, customer relations, and leadership qualities are highly valued. Self-aware individuals are more likely to set realistic career goals and take proactive steps to achieve them. They are aware of their strengths and areas for improvement, allowing them to seek out relevant training and development opportunities. This proactive approach to career development is highly valued in the retail industry, where employees are expected to continuously learn and adapt to changing market trends.

Employees who are self-aware are better equipped to handle the demands of the job. They can effectively manage their emotions, navigate complex social situations, and communicate clearly with customers and colleagues. This ability to understand oneself and others is critical in a fast-paced retail environment where interactions with customers can make or break a sale.

Managers who are self-aware are better able to understand the needs and motivations of their team members, leading to improved morale and productivity. They can also recognize when they need to seek input from others or delegate tasks, leading to more efficient decision-making and team performance.

The purpose of this book is to enlighten you about the significance of self-awareness in your professional growth and to offer practical insights and strategies to help you enhance your self-awareness skills and help you to identify and overcome behaviors that may be holding you back.

Relax and let's embark on the journey of self-discovery and continuous improvement together.

ENJOY!

The Fundamentals Of Self Awareness

As said earlier that Self-awareness is a fundamental aspect of personal development and career advancement which involves the ability to introspect and understand one's own thoughts, feelings, and behaviors. Self-awareness is not a singular trait but encompasses various aspects, which I will be sharing with us:

1. Emotional Self-Awareness: This aspect involves recognizing and understanding one's own emotions. It includes being able to identify a wide range of emotions, from subtle to intense, and understanding the triggers and patterns behind these emotions. Emotional self-awareness enables individuals to manage their emotions effectively, leading to better decision-making and interpersonal relationships.

2. Social Self-Awareness: Social self-awareness refers to the ability to understand how one is perceived by others. It involves being attuned to social cues, such as body language and tone of voice, and recognizing the impact of one's behavior on others. Social self-awareness is crucial in building and maintaining positive relationships, both personally and professionally.
3. Cognitive Self-Awareness: Cognitive self-awareness involves understanding one's own thoughts, beliefs, and cognitive processes. It includes being aware of cognitive biases and distortions that may affect one's perception of reality. Cognitive self-awareness is important for critical thinking, problem-solving, and decision-making, as it allows individuals to recognize and challenge their own assumptions.
4. Physical Self-Awareness: Physical self-awareness pertains to being aware of one's own body and physical sensations. It involves recognizing physical cues, such as tension or discomfort, and understanding the connection between physical and emotional states. Physical self-awareness can contribute to better stress management and overall well-being.
5. Spiritual Self-Awareness: Some individuals also consider spiritual self-awareness as an

important aspect of self-awareness. This involves understanding one's values, beliefs, and purpose in life. Spiritual self-awareness can provide a sense of meaning and direction, guiding one's decisions and actions.

HOW TO DEVELOP SELF-AWARENESS AND WHY IT IS CRUCIAL FOR PERSONAL GROWTH

Developing self-awareness is a crucial step in personal growth and is essential for individuals in any industry, including retail, it is a continuous process that requires commitment and effort. By taking the time to understand their own thoughts, emotions, and behaviors, individuals in the retail industry can position themselves for success and personal growth.

Here are some key points to consider when developing self-awareness and its importance:

Understanding Your Emotions: Self-awareness begins with recognizing and understanding your emotions. This includes being able to identify different emotions as you experience them and understanding the triggers that lead to those emotions. For example, in a retail setting, being aware of how you feel when dealing with difficult customers can help you manage your reactions more effectively.

Self-Reflection: Regular self-reflection is a powerful tool for developing self-awareness. Encourage readers to set aside time to reflect on their thoughts, feelings, and actions. Journaling can be a helpful practice, as it allows individuals to track patterns in their behavior and emotions over time.

Seeking Feedback: Feedback from others can provide valuable insights into how we are perceived by others. Encourage readers to seek feedback from colleagues, mentors, or supervisors, and to be open to constructive criticism. In the retail industry, feedback from customers can also be valuable in understanding how your actions impact others.

Mindfulness Practices: Mindfulness involves being fully present and aware of the present moment. Practices such as meditation, yoga, or simply taking a few minutes each day to focus on your breath can help develop mindfulness and self-awareness.

Personality Assessments: Personality assessments such as the Myers-Briggs Type Indicator (MBTI) or the Big Five Personality Traits can provide insights into your personality and behavior. While these assessments are not definitive, they can be a useful starting point for self-reflection and self-discovery.

Cultivating Empathy: Empathy is the ability to understand and share the feelings of others. Developing empathy can help individuals become more aware of how their actions impact those around them. Encourage readers to practice empathy in their interactions with others, both in and out of the workplace.

Setting Goals: Setting personal development goals can help individuals become more self-aware. Set specific, measurable goals related to their personal and professional growth, and to regularly assess their progress towards those goals.

COMMON OBSTACLES TO SELF-AWARENESS

Self-awareness, while invaluable for personal development, can be hindered by various obstacles. These barriers often prevent individuals from gaining a clear understanding of their thoughts, feelings, and behaviors, limiting their ability to grow and excel in their careers. In the context of the retail industry, these obstacles can be particularly impactful, as they may impede progress towards higher-level roles. Some common barriers to self-awareness include:

Lack of Reflection Time: In the fast-paced environment of retail, employees and managers alike may struggle to find time for introspection. The constant demands of the job can leave little room for deep self-reflection, leading to a superficial understanding of oneself.

External Distractions: The retail environment is often filled with distractions, from customer interactions to inventory management. These external stimuli can make it challenging to focus inward and truly assess one's thoughts and emotions.

Limited Feedback: In some retail settings, feedback may be scarce or ineffective. Without constructive feedback from peers, supervisors, or customers, individuals may struggle to gain insight into their strengths and areas for improvement.

Fear of Failure: The fear of failure can be pervasive in the retail industry, where performance metrics and sales targets are often closely monitored. This fear can prevent individuals from taking risks or exploring new opportunities for growth.

Cultural Norms: In some retail environments, there may be cultural norms that discourage introspection or emotional expression. This can create a barrier to self-awareness, as individuals may feel pressure to conform to external expectations.

Stress and Burnout: The high-stress nature of retail work can contribute to burnout, which can cloud one's ability to reflect on their thoughts and behaviors. Chronic stress can also impact mental health, further hindering self-awareness.

Overconfidence: On the other end of the spectrum, some individuals in the retail industry may exhibit overconfidence, which can lead to a lack of self-awareness. This can prevent them from recognizing areas where they need to improve.

To overcome these obstacles, individuals in the retail industry can benefit from setting aside dedicated time for self-reflection, seeking feedback from trusted sources, and actively working to manage stress and burnout. By addressing these barriers, individuals can enhance their self-awareness and unlock their full potential in their careers.

The Impact Of Self-Awareness On Career Growth

Self-awareness plays a pivotal role in career growth, particularly in the retail industry where interpersonal skills and leadership abilities are highly valued. By understanding oneself better, you can effectively navigate your career paths, make informed decisions, and capitalize on their strengths. **Here are some key ways in which self-awareness can positively impact one's career:**

- **Enhanced Decision Making:** Self-aware individuals are better at making informed decisions about their career paths. They understand their strengths, weaknesses, values, and goals, allowing them to make choices that align with their aspirations.
- **Clarity of Goals:** Self-aware individuals are better able to identify their career goals and aspirations. They have a clear

understanding of what they want to achieve and can align their actions and decisions accordingly.

- **Improved Communication:** Self-awareness leads to better communication skills. Individuals who understand their communication style and how it affects others can effectively convey their ideas, collaborate with colleagues, and build strong professional relationships.
- **Emotional Intelligence:** Self-aware individuals have high emotional intelligence, enabling them to manage their emotions and understand the emotions of others. This skill is crucial in retail, where dealing with diverse personalities is common.
- **Effective Leadership:** Self-awareness is a key trait of successful leaders. Leaders who are aware of their emotions, behaviors, and impact on others can lead with empathy, inspire their teams, and drive positive change within their organizations.
- **Conflict Resolution:** Self-awareness helps in managing conflicts constructively. Individuals who are aware of their triggers and emotional responses can navigate conflicts with colleagues, clients, or stakeholders more effectively, leading to better outcomes.

- **Adaptability and Resilience:** Self-aware individuals are more adaptable to change and resilient in the face of challenges. They can assess situations objectively, learn from setbacks, and bounce back stronger, which is essential in dynamic industries like retail.
- **Career Satisfaction:** Self-awareness leads to greater career satisfaction. Individuals who understand their passions and values can pursue careers that align with them, leading to a more fulfilling professional life.

To understand better how self-awareness is very crucial when it comes to ones career growth, permit me to share you a real life story of an individual who have benefited from improved self-awareness.

Emily had been working in the retail industry for several years, steadily climbing the ranks from a sales associate to a store manager. Despite her hard work and dedication, she felt stuck in her career, unable to move to the next level of leadership.

One day, during a leadership training workshop, Emily was introduced to the concept of self-awareness. She learned that self-awareness is the ability to recognize and understand her own emotions, thoughts, and values, and how they impact her behavior and decisions. She realized that she had been overlooking the importance of self-awareness in her career. She had always been focused on achieving her goals and meeting targets, but she had never taken the time to reflect on her own strengths, weaknesses, and areas for improvement.

Determined to make a change, Emily started practicing self-awareness in her daily life. She began to pay more attention to her emotions and how they influenced her interactions with her team and colleagues. She also started seeking feedback from others to gain a better understanding of how she was perceived in the workplace.

As Emily became more self-aware, she noticed significant improvements in her leadership skills. She was able to communicate more effectively with her team, resolve conflicts more efficiently, and make better decisions. Her colleagues and superiors began to take notice of her transformation and started to entrust her with more responsibilities.

Eventually, she was promoted to a senior leadership position within the company. Her journey to success was not just about her hard work and dedication, but also about her willingness to look inward and understand herself better. Through self-awareness, Emily was able to unlock her full potential and achieve her career goals.

SOME PRACTICAL EXERCISES AND TECHNIQUES TO ENHANCE SELF-AWARENESS

- **Journaling:** Keep a journal to record your thoughts, emotions, and experiences. This

can help you identify patterns in your behavior and gain insights into your thought processes.
- **Mindfulness Meditation:** Practice mindfulness meditation by focusing on the present moment without judgment. This can help you become more aware of your thoughts and feelings.
- **Self-Reflection:** Set aside time for self-reflection regularly. Ask yourself questions like "What are my strengths and weaknesses?" and "How do my actions align with my values?"
- **360-Degree Feedback:** Seek feedback from colleagues, supervisors, and subordinates to gain a more comprehensive view of yourself. This can help you identify blind spots and areas for improvement.
- **Personality Assessments:** Take personality assessments, such as the Myers-Briggs Type Indicator (MBTI) or the Big Five personality traits, to gain a better understanding of your personality traits and how they impact your behavior.
- **Emotional Intelligence (EI) Training**: Develop skills in recognizing and managing your emotions, as well as understanding the emotions of others, through EI training.

- **Self-Compassion Practices:** Treat yourself with kindness and understanding, especially when facing setbacks or challenges.
- **Body Scan:** Practice a body scan meditation, focusing on each part of your body and noting any sensations or tension. This can help you become more aware of how your body responds to stress and emotions.
- **Feedback Loop:** Create a feedback loop where you regularly review your actions and outcomes to see if they align with your intentions and goals.
- **Values Clarification:** Clarify your core values and how they guide your behavior and decisions.

Some self-reflection prompts and activities tailored for professionals in the retail sector to enhance their self-awareness:

Customer Interactions Reflection: Reflect on recent interactions with customers. Consider how your behavior, attitude, and communication style may have influenced the outcome of these interactions. What did you do well, and what could you improve upon?

Team Dynamics Reflection: Think about your interactions with colleagues and team members. How do you contribute to the team dynamic? Are there any patterns in your behavior that may impact team morale or productivity?

Handling Difficult Situations: Recall a challenging situation you faced at work. How did you react? Were there any underlying emotions driving your behavior? How could you have handled the situation differently?

Time Management Reflection: Reflect on how you manage your time and priorities at work. Are there any tasks or activities that consistently take up more time than necessary? How could you improve your time management skills?

Feedback Reception: Consider how you receive feedback from others. Are you open to constructive criticism, or do you tend to become defensive? How can you create a more conducive environment for receiving feedback?

Conflict Resolution: Think about how you approach conflict resolution in the workplace. Do you tend to avoid conflict, or do you address it head-on? How could you improve your conflict resolution skills?

Work-Life Balance: Reflect on your work-life balance. Are you able to disconnect from work and recharge? How could you create a healthier balance between work and personal life?

Career Goals: Consider your long-term career goals. Are you on track to achieve them? What steps can you take to further your professional development and advance in your career?

Values Alignment: Reflect on your core values and how they align with your work. Are there any values that are particularly important to you in your career? How do you demonstrate these values in your work?

Learning and Growth: Think about how you approach learning and growth opportunities. Are you proactive in seeking out new skills and knowledge? How can you continue to develop professionally?

These self-reflection prompts and activities can help professionals in the retail sector deepen your self-awareness and make positive changes in your personal and professional lives.

Overcoming Blind Spots

Self-awareness is not always easy to achieve, as individuals often have blind spots—areas of themselves that they are unaware of or do not fully understand. These blind spots can hinder personal development and career advancement, especially in the dynamic environment of the retail industry. In this section, we will explore strategies for identifying and addressing these blind spots.

1. Seek Feedback: One of the most effective ways to identify blind spots is to seek feedback from others. This can be from colleagues, supervisors, or mentors who can provide valuable insights into your behavior and performance. It's important to be open to constructive criticism and use it as an opportunity for growth.

2. Self-Reflection: Take time to reflect on your thoughts, emotions, and actions. Journaling can be a useful tool for this, allowing you to track patterns and identify areas where you may have blind spots. Consider

questions such as "What triggers my emotions?" or "How do I react in stressful situations?"

3. Assess Your Strengths and Weaknesses: Conduct a self-assessment to identify your strengths and weaknesses. This can help you pinpoint areas where you may have blind spots and need to improve. Use tools like personality assessments or 360-degree feedback to gain a comprehensive view of yourself.

4. Challenge Your Assumptions: We often operate based on assumptions about ourselves and others. Take time to challenge these assumptions and consider alternative perspectives. This can help you uncover blind spots and broaden your understanding of yourself and the world around you.

5. Mindfulness Practices: Engaging in mindfulness practices can help you become more aware of your thoughts, emotions, and behaviors. Techniques such as meditation, yoga, or deep breathing exercises can enhance your self-awareness and help you identify blind spots.

6. Professional Development: Invest in your professional development by seeking out training, workshops, or coaching that can help you enhance your self-awareness. These opportunities can provide you with new insights and tools for addressing blind spots.

7. Regular Check-ins: Schedule regular check-ins with yourself to assess your progress in addressing blind spots. Set goals for improvement and track your development over time. Celebrate your successes and use setbacks as learning opportunities.

Here are some tips for seeking feedback and conducting self-assessment
Seeking Feedback

- **Be Specific:** When requesting feedback, be specific about what you want to know. Ask targeted questions related to your performance, behavior, or areas you're seeking to improve.
- **Choose the Right People:** Seek feedback from individuals who are familiar with your work and can provide honest and constructive criticism. This could include colleagues, supervisors, mentors, or industry experts.
- **Create a Safe Environment: Ensure** that the feedback process is conducted in a safe and non-threatening environment. Encourage honest and open communication, and be receptive to feedback, whether positive or negative.
- **Ask for Examples:** When receiving feedback, ask for specific examples to help you better understand the context and nature of the feedback. This can provide valuable insights into your behavior and performance.
- **Listen Actively:** Listen attentively to the feedback without interrupting or becoming defensive. Take notes if necessary and ask

clarifying questions to ensure you fully understand the feedback.
- **Reflect on the Feedback:** After receiving feedback, take time to reflect on the information. Consider how the feedback aligns with your self-perception and identify areas where you may need to make changes.
- **Follow Up:** Follow up with the individual who provided feedback to thank them for their input and discuss any actions you plan to take based on the feedback.

Self-Assessment

- **Set Clear Goals:** Before conducting a self-assessment, set clear goals for what you want to achieve. Identify specific areas you want to assess and what outcomes you're aiming for.
- **Use a Structured Approach:** Use a structured approach to self-assessment, such as a self-assessment tool or framework. This can help you organize your thoughts and identify areas for improvement.
- **Be Honest and Objective:** Be honest with yourself during the self-assessment process. Acknowledge your strengths and weaknesses without judgment or bias.
- **Gather Feedback from Others:** In addition to self-assessment, seek feedback

from others to gain a more comprehensive view of your performance and behavior.
- **Identify Patterns and Trends:** Look for patterns and trends in your behavior and performance. Identify recurring issues or challenges that may indicate areas for improvement.
- **Develop an Action Plan:** Based on your self-assessment, develop an action plan for improvement. Set specific, achievable goals and outline steps you will take to address any identified areas for improvement.
- **Regularly Review and Adjust:** Regularly review your progress against your goals and adjust your action plan as needed. Continuously assess your performance and behavior to ensure you're on track for personal development and growth.

BEHAVIORAL PATTERNS AND BLIND SPOTS

Behavioral patterns are like breadcrumbs left behind by our subconscious minds, offering clues to our blind spots. These patterns are often habitual and can be observed in how we react, communicate, or make decisions in various situations. Recognizing and understanding these patterns can lead to profound insights into our blind spots.

Imagine you consistently react defensively during team meetings whenever your ideas are challenged. This defensive reaction could be a sign of a blind spot related to your communication style or your attitude towards criticism. By identifying this pattern, you can start to explore why you react this way and what underlying beliefs or insecurities may be contributing to this behavior.

To uncover the blind spot, reflect on past situations where this defensive reaction occurred. Ask yourself:

What triggered this reaction?

How did I feel during the interaction?

What thoughts or assumptions were running through my mind?

Did this reaction align with my intentions or the outcome I desired?

Through this reflection, you might discover that you have a fear of failure or a deep-seated need for approval. This blind spot could be hindering your ability to communicate effectively and collaborate with others.

Once you've identified the blind spot, you can take steps to address it. This may involve:

1. Practicing self-awareness in real-time situations to recognize when you're falling into the old pattern.
2. Seeking feedback from colleagues or mentors to gain a different perspective on your behavior.
3. Engaging in communication or assertiveness training to improve your response in challenging situations.

4. Cultivating a growth mindset to embrace feedback and see it as an opportunity for learning and improvement.

Identifying recurring behavioral patterns can be a powerful tool for uncovering blind spots and fostering personal growth. By paying attention to these patterns and exploring their underlying causes, you can enhance your self-awareness and develop more effective ways of interacting with others.

COGNITIVE BIASES AND BLIND SPOTS

Cognitive biases are systematic patterns of deviation from norm or rationality in judgment, whereby inferences about other people and situations may be drawn in an illogical fashion. These biases can lead to blind spots areas of our thinking where we are unaware or where our perceptions are distorted. Let's explore common cognitive biases and discuss how awareness of these biases can help mitigate their impact on decision-making and self-awareness.

1. Confirmation Bias: Confirmation bias is the tendency to search for, interpret, favor, and recall information in a way that confirms one's preexisting beliefs or hypotheses. In the context of self-awareness, confirmation bias can lead us to seek out information that validates our self-perceptions while ignoring or discounting contradictory evidence. By being aware of this bias, we can actively seek out diverse perspectives and information that challenge our beliefs, helping us to overcome blind spots.

2. Dunning-Kruger Effect: The Dunning-Kruger effect is a cognitive bias in which people with low ability at a task overestimate their ability. This bias can lead to overconfidence and a lack of self-awareness about one's limitations. By understanding the Dunning-Kruger effect, individuals can approach their own competence more humbly, seek out feedback from others, and engage in continuous learning to improve their self-awareness.

3. Anchoring Bias: Anchoring bias is the tendency to rely too heavily on the first piece of information encountered (the "anchor") when making decisions. In the context of self-awareness, anchoring bias can lead us to fixate on initial impressions or information about ourselves, ignoring subsequent information that may provide a more accurate picture. By being aware of this bias, we can actively seek out additional information and perspectives to avoid being anchored to a narrow view of ourselves.

4. Availability Heuristic: The availability heuristic is a mental shortcut that relies on immediate examples that come to mind when evaluating a topic or making a decision. This bias can lead us to overestimate the importance of information that is readily available, such as recent events or vivid experiences, while overlooking less memorable but equally relevant information. By being aware of this bias, we can take a more deliberate and comprehensive approach to self-assessment, considering a broader range of experiences and information.

5. Self-Serving Bias: Self-serving bias is the tendency to attribute positive events to our own character or abilities but attribute negative events to external factors. This bias can lead to a distorted view of oneself, where successes are overemphasized and failures are minimized. By recognizing this bias, individuals can take a more balanced and objective view of their achievements and setbacks, leading to a more accurate self-assessment.

6. Overcoming Cognitive Biases: To overcome cognitive biases and reduce blind spots, individuals can employ strategies such as seeking out diverse perspectives, engaging in critical thinking and reflection, being open to feedback, and actively challenging their own assumptions and beliefs. By developing these habits, individuals can improve their decision-making and enhance their self-awareness, leading to personal growth and development.

LEARNING FROM MISTAKES

One of the most powerful ways to overcome blind spots is by learning from mistakes and setbacks. When we acknowledge and reflect on past failures, we can gain valuable insights that lead to personal growth and increased self-awareness.

Let me share to you how important learning from mistakes is and how it can help us overcome blind spots

1. Acknowledging Mistakes: The first step in learning from mistakes is to acknowledge them. This requires humility and a willingness to admit when we have not succeeded. By acknowledging our mistakes, we can begin to understand where our blind spots may lie.

2. Reflecting on Failures: Reflecting on past failures allows us to gain a deeper understanding of why things went wrong. We can consider what factors contributed to the failure, what we could have done differently, and what we have learned from the experience.

3. Extracting Lessons: Every mistake or failure contains valuable lessons. By extracting these lessons, we can gain new insights into ourselves and our behavior. We can identify patterns or behaviors that may be holding us back and take steps to address them.

4. Cultivating Resilience: Learning from mistakes also helps us cultivate resilience. When we can bounce back from failures and setbacks, we become more confident in our abilities and more willing to take risks. This resilience is key to overcoming blind spots and achieving personal growth.

5. Adjusting Behavior: The ultimate goal of learning from mistakes is to adjust our behavior accordingly. Armed with new insights and lessons, we can take proactive steps to avoid repeating the same mistakes. This may involve changing our approach, seeking out new experiences, or challenging our assumptions.

6. Fostering a Growth Mindset: Embracing a growth mindset is essential in learning from mistakes. Instead of viewing failures as permanent setbacks, we see them as opportunities for growth and development. This mindset shift allows us to approach challenges with optimism and resilience.

7. Seeking Feedback: In the process of learning from mistakes, seeking feedback from others can be invaluable. Others may have insights or perspectives that we have not considered, helping us to gain a more complete understanding of our blind spots.

By emphasizing the value of learning from mistakes, we can encourage personal growth and increased self-awareness. Each mistake is an opportunity to learn and improve, bringing us closer to overcoming our blind spots and achieving our full potential.

Self-Awareness In Leadership

Leadership in the retail sector presents a unique set of challenges and responsibilities. Unlike traditional leadership roles, retail leaders must navigate a dynamic and customer-centric environment while managing diverse teams and driving business growth. In this section, we will explore the distinct aspects of leadership in retail and the importance of self-awareness in meeting these challenges.

Retail leaders face the challenge of balancing customer satisfaction with operational efficiency. They must make strategic decisions to enhance the shopping experience while ensuring profitability. Additionally, retail leaders often deal with high employee turnover rates and the need to motivate and engage their teams effectively. They are responsible for setting the vision and direction for their teams, aligning their efforts with the overall business goals. They must also manage day-to-day operations, including inventory management, sales strategies, and customer service. Furthermore, retail leaders play a crucial role in developing and mentoring their team members to achieve their full potential.

The Role of Self-Awareness in Retail Leadership is particularly critical for retail leaders as it helps them understand their own strengths, weaknesses, and values. By being self-aware, leaders can make better decisions, communicate effectively, and build stronger relationships with their teams and customers.

The Importance of Self-Awareness for Leaders

Self-awareness is widely recognized as a critical trait for effective leadership, particularly in the fast-paced and competitive retail sector. This brought me to share with you, why self-awareness is essential for leaders and how it can enhance their effectiveness.

1. **Enhanced Decision Making:** Self-aware leaders are better equipped to make sound decisions. By understanding their own values, biases, and motivations, they can make choices that align with their personal and organizational goals. This ability to make informed decisions is particularly valuable in the ever-changing landscape of the retail industry.

1. **Improved Communication and Relationships:** Self-awareness enables leaders to communicate more effectively with their teams and stakeholders. By understanding their own communication styles and how they are perceived by others, leaders can tailor their messages for better clarity and impact. Additionally, self-aware leaders are more empathetic and understanding, which helps them build stronger relationships with their team members and customers.

1. **Authentic Leadership:** Self-awareness leads to more authentic and genuine leadership. When leaders are aware of their strengths and weaknesses, they are more likely to be transparent about their limitations and seek support where needed. This authenticity fosters trust and respect among team members, leading to a more positive and productive work environment.

1. **Personal and Professional Growth:** Self-aware leaders are constantly learning and growing. By regularly reflecting on their

experiences and seeking feedback, they can identify areas for improvement and take proactive steps to develop their skills. This commitment to personal and professional growth not only benefits the leader but also inspires their team members to do the same.

DEVELOPING SELF-AWARENESS IN LEADERSHIP

Practical strategies for leaders to enhance their self-awareness and integrate self-awareness development into their daily leadership practices.

1. Self-Reflection

Set aside time regularly for self-reflection. This can be done through journaling, meditation, or simply taking a few minutes each day to reflect on their thoughts, emotions, and actions. Self-reflection helps to gain insights into your own behavior and decision-making processes.

2. Seeking Feedback

Seek feedback from your peers, mentors, and team members. Feedback can provide valuable insights into blind spots and areas for improvement that leaders may not be aware of. It is important for you as a leader to approach feedback with an open mind and a willingness to learn and grow.

3. Mindfulness Practices

Mindfulness practices, such as meditation and deep breathing exercises, can help to develop greater self-awareness. These practices can help you to become more attuned to your thoughts, emotions, and physical sensations, allowing you to respond more thoughtfully and effectively in challenging situations.

4. Emotional Intelligence Training

Emotional intelligence training can help in understanding your own emotions and how they impact your behavior, as well as how to effectively manage their emotions in various situations.

5. Integrating Self-Awareness into Daily Practices

Integrate self-awareness development into your daily leadership practices. For example, they can start meetings with a brief mindfulness exercise or take a few minutes at the end of each day to reflect on their interactions and decisions. By making self-awareness a priority in their daily routines, leaders can continue to strengthen this important skill.

CHALLENGES AND PITFALLS IN DEVELOPING SELF-AWARENESS

While developing self-awareness is crucial for effective leadership, leaders may encounter several challenges and pitfalls along the way. It's important for leaders to be aware of these challenges so they can address them effectively.

1. Ego: One of the biggest challenges to self-awareness is the ego. Ego can cloud judgment and prevent leaders from seeing their own weaknesses or limitations.

It's important for leaders to recognize when their ego is at play and be willing to set it aside in order to see themselves more clearly.

2. Blind Spots: Another common challenge is blind spots, which are areas of our personality or behavior that we are unaware of. Blind spots can prevent leaders from recognizing the impact of their actions on others or understanding how others perceive them. Seeking feedback from others can help leaders uncover blind spots and work to address them.

3. Fear of Failure: Leaders may also face a fear of failure when it comes to developing self-awareness. They may be afraid to confront their weaknesses or past mistakes, fearing that it will undermine their leadership credibility. It's important for leaders to embrace failure as a learning opportunity and not be afraid to acknowledge their shortcomings.

4. Lack of Time: In the fast-paced retail environment, leaders may struggle to find the time for self-reflection and introspection. However, developing self-awareness requires dedicated time and effort. Leaders should prioritize self-awareness development and carve out time in their schedule for reflection and self-assessment.

5. Resistance to Change: Finally, leaders may face resistance to change when it comes to developing self-awareness. Change can be uncomfortable, and leaders may be reluctant to step out of their comfort zone. However, embracing change is essential for personal and professional growth.

By being aware of common challenges such as ego, blind spots, fear of failure, lack of time, and resistance to change, leaders can take proactive steps to overcome these obstacles and continue to grow and develop as leaders.

Developing self-awareness is not just a personal journey; it is a critical step towards becoming an effective leader, especially in the dynamic world of retail. Despite the challenges and pitfalls that may arise, the benefits of self-awareness enhanced decision-making, improved communication, and authentic leadership are well worth the effort. By embracing self-reflection, seeking feedback, practicing mindfulness, and addressing common challenges such as ego and blind spots, leaders can cultivate a deeper understanding of themselves and their impact on others. This journey of self-discovery is not always easy, but it is essential for personal and professional growth.

As leaders in the retail sector, developing self-awareness is not just beneficial for ourselves, but for our teams, our organizations, and the customers we serve.

Cultural And Gender Perspectives On Self-Awareness

Different cultures emphasize various aspects of the self, such as individuality, collectivism, or spirituality, which can influence how individuals perceive themselves. For example, in cultures that prioritize collectivism, individuals may define themselves more in relation to their family or community, leading to a different sense of self-awareness compared to cultures that emphasize individualism. Cultural values regarding self-expression, emotional expression, and assertiveness can impact how individuals communicate their thoughts, feelings, and needs. Some cultures may encourage more reserved or indirect forms of self-expression, while others may value directness and assertiveness.

Cultural attitudes towards personal growth and development can influence individuals' willingness to engage in self-reflection and introspection. Cultures that value continuous improvement may foster a stronger sense of self-awareness compared to cultures that prioritize conformity or stability. In diverse cultural environments, individuals may navigate multiple cultural influences, leading to a more complex and nuanced sense of self-awareness. Understanding and embracing cultural diversity can enhance self-awareness by encouraging individuals to consider different perspectives and worldviews, a culture of inclusivity and respect for diversity can promote greater self-awareness and understanding among team members.

In collectivist cultures, such as many Asian, African, and South American societies, the emphasis is often on the group rather than the individual. This can have a significant impact on self-awareness, as individuals may define themselves more in terms of their relationships and roles within the group rather than as autonomous individuals. **Here are some reasons to consider:**

- **Group Identity vs. Individual Identity:** In collectivist cultures, individuals are more likely to see themselves as part of a larger social unit, such as their family, community, or nation. This strong sense of group identity can lead to a lower emphasis on individual self-awareness, as the focus is on maintaining harmony within the group.
- **Role of Social Norms and Expectations:** Social norms and expectations in collectivist cultures may dictate how individuals perceive themselves

and their place within the group. Individuals may prioritize fulfilling societal roles and obligations over personal introspection and self-exploration.
- **Impact on Communication Styles**: In collectivist cultures, communication styles may be more indirect and context dependent, as individuals strive to maintain group harmony. This can influence how individuals express their thoughts, feelings, and self-perceptions, affecting their self-awareness.

To Develop Self-Awareness in Collectivist Cultures; Reflect on how your actions and decisions impact the group as a whole. Promote activities that foster empathy and understanding of others' perspectives, which can enhance self-awareness within a collectivist framework. Contrasting collectivist cultures with individualistic cultures can provide valuable insights into the different ways self-awareness is understood and cultivated around the world.

Cultural attitudes towards emotions, self-expression, and social hierarchy can significantly impact an individual's self-awareness. In many cultures, the expression of emotions is influenced by societal norms and expectations. For example, in some cultures, there may be an emphasis on emotional restraint, leading individuals to suppress their emotions and potentially inhibit their self-awareness. Conversely, in cultures that encourage emotional expression, individuals may be more in tune with their emotions, leading to a deeper level of self-awareness.

Similarly, cultural attitudes towards self-expression can shape how individuals perceive and communicate their thoughts and feelings. In some cultures, there may be an emphasis on modesty and humility, which can impact how individuals present themselves to others and how they reflect on their own thoughts and behaviors. In contrast, cultures that value assertiveness and self-promotion may encourage individuals to be more vocal about their thoughts and feelings, potentially leading to a greater sense of self-awareness.

Social hierarchy within a culture can also influence self-awareness. In cultures with strict hierarchies, individuals may be more attuned to their position within the social structure, which can affect how they perceive themselves in relation to others. This awareness of social status can impact self-esteem and self-perception, influencing overall self-awareness.

Cultural attitudes towards emotions, self-expression, and social hierarchy can shape an individual's self-awareness by influencing how they perceive and interpret their own thoughts, feelings, and behaviors in relation to the world around them.

GENDER DIFFERENCES IN SELF-AWARENESS

Gender differences in self-awareness are often influenced by societal expectations and stereotypes. Research suggests that women may be more attuned to their emotions and interpersonal relationships compared to men. This difference in self-awareness styles can be attributed to various factors, including socialization, cultural norms, and biological differences.

Societal expectations play a significant role in shaping how men and women perceive and express their self-awareness. For example, traditional gender roles often dictate that men should be stoic and unemotional, while women are expected to be nurturing and empathetic. These stereotypes can create barriers for men and women in developing a balanced and holistic sense of self-awareness. Men may feel pressure to suppress their emotions or ignore their emotional needs, leading to a limited understanding of their inner world. On the other hand, women may face expectations to prioritize others' feelings over their own, which can impact their ability to assert their needs and boundaries.

To navigate these societal expectations and stereotypes, individuals can benefit from challenging gender norms and embracing a more inclusive and fluid understanding of gender roles. By recognizing and valuing the unique experiences and perspectives of individuals of all genders, we can create a more supportive and empowering environment for everyone to develop their self-awareness.

It's essential to recognize that self-awareness is a personal journey that is influenced by a variety of factors, including gender. By acknowledging and understanding these differences, individuals can cultivate a deeper sense of self-awareness that is authentic and empowering, regardless of gender.

Navigating cultural and gender differences in self-awareness requires a nuanced approach. **Here's how you can effectively manage these challenges:**

- **Mindfulness of Cultural Background:** Reflect on their cultural upbringing and how it shapes their self-awareness. Suggest keeping an open mind and being willing to explore different cultural perspectives.
- **Empathy and Understanding:** Stress the importance of empathy in understanding others' perspectives. Listen actively and without judgment, seeking to understand the cultural and gender influences behind others' behaviors.
- **Cultural Competence:** Develop cultural competence by educating yourself about different cultures and genders. This includes learning about cultural norms, values, and communication styles.
- **Respectful Communication:** use language and communication styles that are respectful of different cultural and gender identities, be open to feedback and be willing to adjust your communication approach as needed.

- **Seeking Diverse Perspectives:** seek out diverse perspectives and experiences, this can include engaging in conversations with individuals from different cultural backgrounds and actively seeking out literature and media that represent diverse voices.
- **Continuous Learning:** Regularly assess your own biases and assumptions, and seek opportunities for personal growth and development in this area.

Here are some practical tips for developing cultural competence and gender sensitivity in professional interactions:

Cultural Competence:

Educate yourself about different cultures, including their customs, traditions, and communication styles.

Avoid making assumptions based on stereotypes and be open-minded when encountering cultural differences.

Seek opportunities to interact with individuals from diverse backgrounds to broaden your cultural understanding.

Practice active listening and show respect for differing viewpoints and practices.

Be willing to adapt your communication style and behavior to accommodate cultural differences.

Gender Sensitivity:

Be aware of gender biases and stereotypes that may influence your perceptions and interactions.

Treat all individuals with respect and avoid making assumptions based on gender.

Encourage gender diversity and inclusivity in the workplace by supporting initiatives that promote equality.

Create a work environment that is inclusive and respectful of all genders, where everyone feels valued and supported.

Be mindful of language use and avoid language that may be perceived as gender-biased or exclusive.

Building Relationships Across Cultures and Genders:

Focus on building trust and rapport with individuals from diverse backgrounds.

Take the time to understand the perspectives and experiences of others, especially those from different cultures and genders.

Be empathetic and considerate of cultural and gender differences in your interactions.

Use inclusive language and gestures to ensure that everyone feels included and respected.

Seek feedback from colleagues and peers to gain insights into how your behavior may be perceived across different cultures and genders.

By implementing these strategies, you can enhance your cultural competence and gender sensitivity, leading to more effective and respectful professional interactions.

SELF-AWARENESS IN CONFLICT RESOLUTION

Self-awareness plays a crucial role in conflict resolution, especially in the workplace. When individuals are self-aware, they are better able to understand their own emotions, motivations, and reactions, which can help them navigate conflicts more effectively. **Here are some ways self-awareness can aid in conflict resolution:**

Emotional Regulation: Self-aware individuals are better equipped to regulate their emotions during conflicts. They can identify when they are becoming upset or agitated and take steps to calm themselves down before responding.

Empathy: Self-awareness also fosters empathy, the ability to understand and share the feelings of another. When individuals are aware of their own emotions, they are more likely to empathize with the emotions of others, which is essential for resolving conflicts peacefully.

Communication: Self-aware individuals are often better communicators. They can express their thoughts and feelings clearly and assertively, which can help prevent misunderstandings that can lead to conflicts.

Conflict Resolution Styles: Self-awareness can help individuals identify their preferred conflict resolution styles. For example, some people may prefer to avoid conflicts altogether, while others may confront conflicts head-on. Understanding these preferences can help individuals choose the most appropriate approach for resolving conflicts.

Practical Tips for Handling Conflicts in the Workplace:

- **Listen Actively:** During conflicts, it's essential to listen actively to the other person's perspective. Avoid interrupting and try to understand their point of view.
- **Focus on Solutions:** Instead of dwelling on the problem, focus on finding a solution that is acceptable to all parties involved. Brainstorming together can lead to creative solutions.
- **Stay Calm:** It's natural to feel upset during conflicts, but try to stay calm and composed. Take a few deep breaths or step away for a moment if necessary.
- **Use "I" Statements:** When expressing your feelings and concerns, use "I" statements to avoid sounding accusatory. For example, say, "I feel frustrated when..." instead of "You always..."
- **Seek Mediation if Necessary:** If conflicts cannot be resolved directly, consider seeking mediation from a neutral third party, such as a manager or HR representative.

The Journey Of Self-Discovery And Continuous Improvement

Embarking on a journey of self-discovery can be a transformative experience, offering numerous benefits that can positively impact every aspect of your life. One of the key advantages of self-discovery is increased self-awareness. By exploring your thoughts, emotions, and motivations, you gain a deeper understanding of yourself, which can lead to greater self-acceptance and confidence. Self-discovery also enhances decision-making skills. When you have a clear understanding of your values, goals, and priorities, you can make choices that align with your authentic self, leading to more fulfilling outcomes. Additionally, self-discovery can improve your relationships. By understanding yourself better, you can communicate more effectively, empathize with others, and form deeper connections.

The journey of self-discovery is not only about understanding who you are but also about becoming the best version of yourself. It can lead to personal growth, resilience, and a deeper sense of purpose and fulfillment in life. So, embrace this journey with an open mind and heart, and you may be surprised at the incredible discoveries you make along the way.

let's talk about Jane, a retail manager who felt stuck in her career. She was constantly passed over for promotions, and despite her hard work, she couldn't understand why. One day, she decided to embark on a journey of self-discovery. She started by reflecting on her strengths, weaknesses, and values, and soon she began to see herself in a new light. Jane realized that she had been holding herself back by not speaking up in meetings and not taking risks. Armed with this new self-awareness, she began to make changes. She started voicing her ideas, taking on new challenges, and seeking feedback. Slowly but surely, Jane's career began to flourish. She was promoted to a senior director role, and she finally felt fulfilled in her work.

Self-discovery is the greatest adventure; you never know what treasures you may find within yourself, By embarking on a journey of self-discovery, you open yourself up to a world of possibilities. You may uncover hidden talents, rediscover forgotten passions, or gain a newfound appreciation for who you are. So, take that first step, and who knows where your journey may lead you.

SETTING PERSONAL DEVELOPMENT GOALS

Setting personal development goals is a crucial step in enhancing self-awareness and achieving growth, both personally and professionally. By following the SMART criteria Specific, Measurable, Achievable, Relevant, and Time-bound you can ensure that your goals are well-defined and actionable. Here's how you can set SMART goals:

Specific: Clearly define what you want to achieve. Instead of a vague goal like "improve communication skills," specify it as "improve public speaking skills to confidently present ideas at team meetings."

Measurable: Determine how you will measure your progress. For example, if your goal is to "increase sales," specify by what percentage or amount you aim to increase them.

Achievable: Ensure that your goal is realistic and attainable. Consider your current skills, resources, and time constraints. Setting a goal to "become a senior director within six months" might not be achievable, but aiming for a promotion within a realistic timeframe could be.

Relevant: Your goal should align with your personal and professional objectives. It should contribute to your overall growth and development. For example, if your long-term goal is to lead a team, setting a goal to "complete a leadership training program" would be relevant.

Time-bound: Set a deadline for achieving your goal. This creates a sense of urgency and helps you stay focused. For instance, "achieve certification in project management within the next year.

Here are some examples of goals that can help individuals progress in their careers:

- **Enhancing Customer Service Skills:** Set a goal to improve customer interactions by implementing strategies to increase customer satisfaction and loyalty.
- **Developing Leadership Skills:** Aim to take on leadership roles or projects that allow you to demonstrate your ability to lead teams effectively.
- **Improving Sales Techniques:** Set targets for increasing sales performance through upselling, cross-selling, and customer relationship building.
- **Enhancing Product Knowledge:** Set a goal to become an expert in the products you sell, including features, benefits, and competitive advantages.
- **Building Networking Skills:** Aim to expand your professional network within the retail industry by attending industry events and connecting with professionals.

- **Developing Time Management Skills:** Set goals to improve your efficiency and productivity, such as reducing time spent on non-essential tasks.
- **Enhancing Communication Skills:** Aim to improve your verbal and written communication skills, including active listening and clarity in conveying messages.
- **Learning New Technologies:** Set a goal to become proficient in using new technologies relevant to the retail industry, such as point-of-sale systems or inventory management software.
- **Seeking Feedback and Mentorship:** Set a goal to actively seek feedback from supervisors, peers, and mentors to identify areas for improvement and growth.
- **Earning Relevant Certifications or Qualifications:** Aim to obtain certifications or qualifications that are recognized in the retail industry and relevant to your career goals.

MINDSET SHIFT FOR GROWTH

Coined by psychologist Carol Dweck, the concept of a growth mindset emphasizes the belief that our abilities and intelligence can be developed through dedication and hard work. In contrast to a fixed mindset, which believes that abilities are innate and unchangeable, a growth mindset thrives on challenges and sees failures as opportunities for growth. This mindset shift is especially relevant in the fast-paced and ever-changing landscape of the retail industry.

By embracing a growth mindset, individuals in the retail sector can cultivate resilience, adaptability, and a passion for learning. They can view setbacks not as permanent barriers but as temporary hurdles on the path to success. This mindset shift encourages individuals to step out of their comfort zones, take calculated risks, and continually seek new opportunities for growth.

A growth mindset fosters a love for learning and a belief in one's ability to improve. It encourages individuals to seek feedback, learn from criticism, and constantly refine their skills. In the retail industry, where innovation and adaptation are key, a growth mindset can be a powerful asset, enabling individuals to navigate challenges and seize opportunities for advancement.

To cultivate a growth mindset, individuals can start by reframing their beliefs about their abilities and embracing challenges as opportunities for growth. They can learn from the success of others, seek out constructive feedback, and celebrate their progress along the way. By adopting a growth mindset, individuals in the retail industry can unlock their full potential and achieve new heights of personal and professional success.

Tips to help individuals develop this mindset:

Embrace Challenges: View challenges as opportunities for growth rather than obstacles. Approach new tasks or projects with a positive attitude, knowing that they offer a chance to learn and improve.

Learn from Feedback: Instead of seeing feedback as criticism, see it as valuable input for improvement. Use feedback to identify areas for growth and development.

Persistence in the Face of Obstacles: Understand that setbacks are a natural part of the learning process. Maintain a positive attitude and persevere through challenges, knowing that effort and persistence lead to improvement.

Emphasize Effort Over Outcome: Focus on the process rather than the outcome. Value the effort and hard work you put into your work, regardless of the final result.

Cultivate Curiosity: Stay curious and open-minded. Seek out new opportunities to learn and grow, both within and outside the retail industry.

Celebrate Growth: Acknowledge and celebrate your progress and achievements, no matter how small. Recognizing your growth reinforces a positive mindset.

Surround Yourself with Growth-Oriented People: Build a network of colleagues, mentors, and friends who support your growth mindset. Learn from their experiences and seek their guidance when needed.

Continuously Learn and Develop: Take advantage of learning opportunities within the retail industry, such as workshops, training programs, and conferences. Stay updated on industry trends and best practices.

As It's important to develop a growth mindset, it's also essential to recognize and appreciate the steps you've taken, no matter how small they may seem.

Here are some ways to acknowledge your progress:

- **Journaling:** Keeping a journal can help you track your progress over time. Write down your thoughts, feelings, and achievements to reflect on how far you've come.
- **Setting Milestones:** Break down your goals into smaller, achievable milestones. Celebrate each milestone you reach as a step forward in your journey.
- **Rewarding Yourself:** Treat yourself to something special as a reward for your hard work. Whether it's a small indulgence or a bigger reward for a major achievement, celebrating your successes can help motivate you to keep going.
- **Sharing Successes:** Share your successes with others, such as friends, family, or colleagues. Celebrating together can not only boost your own morale but also inspire and motivate those around you.
- **Reflecting on Growth:** Take time to reflect on how you've grown and changed throughout your journey. Celebrate the

positive changes you've made and use them as motivation to continue growing.

Remember, celebrating progress is not just about the end goal but also about appreciating the effort and dedication you've put in along the way.

CREATING A PERSONAL DEVELOPMENT PLAN:

To create a personalized development plan, start by identifying your goals and aspirations. Consider where you currently are in your personal and professional life and where you want to be in the future.

Define Your Goals: Clearly define your short-term and long-term goals. Make sure they are specific, measurable, achievable, relevant, and time-bound (SMART goals).

Identify Areas for Improvement: Reflect on areas of your life or career where you feel you could improve. This could include skills, habits, or mindset.

Set Priorities: Determine which goals are most important to you and prioritize them accordingly.

Develop Action Steps: Break down your goals into smaller, manageable steps. Consider what actions you need to take to achieve each goal.

Create a Timeline: Establish a timeline for achieving your goals. Set deadlines for each action step to keep yourself accountable.

Seek Feedback: Share your development plan

with a mentor, coach, or trusted friend. They can provide valuable feedback and support.

Review and Adjust: Regularly review your progress and adjust your plan as needed. Be flexible and willing to adapt to changes.

You can follow this template in developing your Personal Development Plan:

Goal: [Insert your goal here]

Objective: [Outline the specific objective you want to achieve]

Action Steps: [List the steps you will take to achieve your goal]

Timeline: [Set deadlines for each action step]

Resources Needed: [Identify any resources or support you will need]

Progress Tracking: [How will you track your progress?]

Remember that the journey of self-discovery and continuous improvement is not a destination but a lifelong process. As you navigate your career in the retail industry, embrace the opportunities for growth and learning that come your way. Take the first step on this journey with confidence, knowing that with dedication and perseverance, you can achieve your goals and reach new heights of success. Your journey of self-discovery is just beginning, and the possibilities for growth are endless. Embrace this new chapter with enthusiasm and a commitment to your personal and professional development.

Conclusion

Self-awareness is not just a buzzword; it is a powerful tool that can significantly impact your personal and professional life. Throughout this book, we have explored the various facets of self-awareness and its relevance to your career in the retail industry.

By becoming more self-aware, you have the opportunity to identify and overcome obstacles that may be holding you back. You can develop a deeper understanding of your strengths and weaknesses, allowing you to make more informed decisions and navigate your career path with confidence.

As you continue on your journey of self-discovery and personal development, remember that self-awareness is not a destination but a continuous process. Embrace every opportunity to learn more about yourself, seek feedback from others, and challenge yourself to grow.

I encourage you to take the insights and techniques shared in this book and apply them to your daily life. By investing in your self-awareness, you are investing in your future success.

Thank you for joining me on this journey. May you continue to grow, thrive, and achieve your goals in the retail industry and beyond.

About the Author

NaToya Champion was born and raised in Madison, Ms. NaToya considers her family and her faith to be the most important things to her. NaToya values community and fostering positive relationships. If she isn't working. she's enjoying spending time with her loved ones, especially her children.

www.ingramcontent.com/pod-product-compliance
Lightning Source LLC
LaVergne TN
LVHW012243070526
838201LV00090B/109